FOUR SEASONS

Copyright © Younok Dumortier Shin 2020

All rights reserved. No part of this book may be reproduced or used in any manner without the prior written permission of the copyright owner, except for the use of brief quotations in a book review.

To request permissions, contact
younok.dumortiershin@alaired.com

ISBN: 978-0-578-77108-3

Library of Congress Control Number: 2020918615

First edition September 2020
Published by Alaired LLC in the USA.

FOUR SEASONS

By
Younok Dumortier Shin

To You,
Who is listening

Table of Contents

PRELUDE — 2

- VOICES IN MY HEAD — 3
- ONCE UPON A TIME... — 4

SPRING - SPROUT — 5

- GRANDPA AND GRANDDAUGHTER — 6
- COUNTRYSIDE — 7
- SATURDAY CLASS — 8
- LONGING — 9
- WHERE SHE GREW UP — 10
- HIGH SCHOOL GRADUATION — 12
- MOM AND DAD TALKING — 13
- FIRST TIME IN A PLANE — 14
- "GO HOME!" — 16
- TEARS — 17
- YOU WILL SEE — 19

SUMMER - BLOSSOM — 20

- "F" — 21
- BUILDING THE PATH — 23
- 'WHAT DO I WANT TO BE?' — 25
- GRADUATION — 27
- FIRST PAYCHECK — 28
- BRIDE AND GROOM — 30
- JUGGLING — 31
- FINDING PURPOSE — 33
- LIFETIME OPPORTUNITY — 35
- REINVENTING — 36
- CHOCOLATE FOUNTAIN — 38

FALL - WITHER — 39

BIRTHDAY	40
WHEN YOUR SOUL IS SPEAKING TO YOU	42
INSOMNIA	44
WORDS OF WISDOM	45
WHAT HURTS MORE	46
SHE ASKED ME IF	47
LETTER	49
TWO LADIES ON A BENCH	50
RESPECTFUL GOODBYE	52
LAST DAY	54

WINTER - REST — 56

MEDITATION	57
RAINDROPS	58
DESIRE	59
WOULD THAT BE OK	61
VOICE	62
I ALMOST LOST YOU	63
LETTER TO YOU FROM MY OPEN HEART	65
3:00 A.M.	67
RECEIVING LOVE	69
WHEN I AM NO LONGER HERE	71

PRELUDE

Voices in My Head

No, I *can't* write.
Of course, you **can** write.

I was *never* good at writing.
Yet, you have **always** been writing.

Nobody cares about my stories.
Somebody will care about your stories.

I don't know *fancy* words and phrases.
You do know **simple** words and phrases.

Leave me alone! I can never be a *good* writer.
Just write, be **faithful** to your stories.

- **Everyone has stories,**
    stories waiting to be told -

Once Upon a Time...

There was a little girl who had big dreams
Living in a country with many tiny streams.

One day
She left her small country to live in a big country
To feed her desires that were constantly hungry.

As many years passed by
She reached a mountain top
But her heart was beginning to drop.

The farther she climbed
The more she succumbed.

Standing on the mountain crest
She thought she was the best.

Yet others who climbed had the same aim
Her ambition became a dangerous flame.

So, she climbed down, down from that great hill
Holding on to her soul within her still.

Then she lived in a solitary life
Searching for the root of her strife.

SPRING - SPROUT

Grandpa and Granddaughter

My dear,
You need to help your mom.

Mop the floor.
Clean the dishes.
Wash the clothes.

Your mom works day and night.
You really should help her.

Yes, grandpa!

Then
Ten-year-old-granddaughter went away
And took a nap.

Countryside

It is summertime!
It is my country time!
I will visit my cousin's house
In a tiny little country town.

We will swim in the creek.
We will catch the tadpoles.
We will chase the dragonflies.
We will tell ghost stories.

Endless rice field,
Silhouettes of green and yellow,
Cows mooing,
Pigs grunting,
Crickets chirping,
And children singing.

It is summertime!
It is my country time!
I will visit my cousin's house
In a tiny little country town.

Saturday Class

Hey you,
What do you want to do
During our class today?
It's Saturday.
Do you want to skip it?

Yeah, sure.
I am tired of all this school anyway.
Day and night,
Saturdays and Sundays,
To get into a college,
Just to find a good husband.

Where do you want to hang out?
We can't be caught.

We can go to see the airplanes
Taking off and landing.
We can scream our lungs out.
We can dance around like silly.
And no one will be there to find out.

Longing

It was her favorite place.
An open field next to the airport.
Powerful planes roaring with confidence.

She loved sitting there.
Engines thundering
Wind blasting
Her heart throbbing.

'I will be flying all around the world someday!'

Nobody knew her secret.
Where she lived, her future was already laid out.
A good housewife
Living a simple life.

She was lonely.
And sad.
She had a dream - bigger than life.

She loved sitting there
Looking at the planes
Imagining some day

Flying everywhere!

Where She Grew Up

Where she grew up, she did not mean much.

She grew up in a household where
Her brother meant everything.
The only son in the house
Smart one
Successful one
The one who would carry the family name
The one who would inherit everything.

She was much younger than he
Not as smart as he
Inadequate
The one who must find a good husband
The one who would inherit nothing.

She believed her nothingness,
Never smart enough or pretty enough
No chance of success in life.

She was awfully shy
Alone
Depressed.

In the mist of her depression
And nothingness
Something strong inside her
Constantly wriggling:

Curiosity!

She was curious about everything.
Why were we born? Why do we fight? Why are we poor?
Why is the earth tilted? Why do the snakes have no legs?

Her endless questions on
Any topic
Any time of the day
Drove everyone crazy!

She was told to be quiet.
Never to ask many questions.

But the wriggling inside of her
Refused to settle down.

So, she longed to go somewhere
Far away

To learn everything there is to learn
To satisfy her endless questions
That nobody cared to answer

Where she grew up.

High School Graduation

She almost did not go to her high school graduation.
To her, it was nothing special.
'Everyone graduates from high school anyway.'

There were many people
Celebrating their academic accomplishments
Taking pictures
Shaking hands
Carrying colorful flowers and balloons.

She never cared for any of that.
'All that meaningless stuff.'

For years
She longed to leave her small country
To a big country
Where big promises beckoned
Learning all the greatness that life has to offer.

She felt empty.
Stuck.
The graduation with so many happy faces
Made her feel revolted.

*'I must tell my mom and dad tonight.
I have to get out of here!'*

Mom and Dad Talking

She is staying here.
She doesn't want to stay here.

She is a girl, and she can't go anywhere.
She may be a girl, but she wants to go out there.

What she needs is a spouse.
What she needs is a chance.

We can't afford it.
We will find a way to afford it.

Why are you on her side?

Because I was once a girl who never got a chance.

First Time in a Plane

After so many years of longing
She thought she would be thrilled to be in that plane,
The plane that was taking her across the Pacific Ocean
Away from the small country where she grew up.

The flight was different from everything she imagined:
Tiny seats
Cigarette smell (yes, people used to smoke in the planes!)
Untidy people with loud voices
Military-like food tray.

She imagined
Luxury seats
Clean fresh smell
Well-dressed people
Elegant food.

In her young mind, airplanes symbolized success.
Success meant fancy and elegant.

Seeing how different reality was
From her imagination
She realized that
She never thought about what she wanted to become.

She never asked that question till then.
Her only goal was to get on the plane to leave her country.
But doing what now?

In that plane
She saw where she belonged -
Economy class
Tiny, smelly, noisy.

She saw where she wanted to belong -
First class
Spacious, calm, elegant.
ELEGANT!

Yes, that is it.
I want to become a businesswoman
Elegant and powerful
Flying around the world making tons of money.

So, it was like that.
She picked her dream job
Naïvely
The first time she flew in a plane.

"Go Home!"

A foreign student
In a big country
On a student visa
Trying to learn everything,
Trying to fit in.

The mother of a friend,
A friend with whom this foreign student used to hang out
During high school
Back home in her small country
Whose family moved to the big country a few years prior
Who promised to the foreign student
That she would be safe with them.

After six months together

The mother said to the foreign student,

"Go Home! You have no hope here!"

Tears

I am waiting for the downtown bus.
It is raining.
It is cold.

I am burying my puffy eyes
Underneath my winter coat.

I can pretend that
It is the rain
Not the tears
All over my face.

I don't know what I will do in downtown.
Maybe I will look for things for my empty apartment.

I never knew the loneliness like this before.
It is ripping my heart into a million pieces.
Pain
Seeping through my skin
Seeping through my bones.

I miss my mom!
Oh, how I miss her!
I hope she is flying home ok.
It is a long trip across the Pacific Ocean.

She came all this way to check on me.
To make sure I am not doing anything stupid.
That I am studying as hard as I can.

It is a lot of money she is sending
For my education in this country.

She is flying home with a heavy heart.
A person whom we trusted dearly told her
That I have no chance in this country.
That I should go back home.
Because I am a foreign student.
Because I don't even speak good English.

We both cried all through last night.

She cried
Because she was a poor mother from a poor country
Too powerless to defend for her daughter.

I cried
Because I was a poor daughter from a poor country
Too powerless to stand up for myself.

There is something about humiliation.
It changes people.
It is changing me.

Bitterness.

I am burying my face underneath my coat.
It is raining.
It is so cold.

You Will See

I will prove to you

That I can make it

I will shine so bright

I will dazzle you!

SUMMER - BLOSSOM

"F"

The grade she received in her very first college class:
"F"
On her midterm exam
In economics class.

She memorized her textbook day and night.
But the exam had two essay questions.
She could not write much.
She never experienced essay exams before.
Where she grew up
The exams were multiple-choice questions.

Her paper had the teacher's note
Next to the big letter **"F"**
In a bright red color

"I highly recommend that
You take more English as Second Language classes
Before continuing."

Flashing on her face
Telling her
You Can't Make It!

She felt her life was finished.
Miserable failure.
Never smart enough to be useful in this world.
As many people had told her.

Then
Something arose inside of her:
Boldness.

I am already a failure,
So, what difference does it make
If I fail one more time?

She continued on.

She studied differently for her final exam.
She created possible exam questions.
And she created the answers.

Writing away her essays
Day and night
Paper after paper
Editing
Revising
Perfecting.

She received a 'B' as her final course grade.

This became her guiding principle.

Being a failure comes with freedom.
Freedom to try the impossible.

Building the Path

One thing about her college days:
She was always hungry.

On a student visa,
She received the money from her parents
For her tuition and all living expenses.
Her parents saved the money for her
While making their ends met.

They always reminded her of that:
She was very expensive
She hadn't proved that she was worth it
She owed them every single penny they were sending her.

She lived with guilt.
She tried to cut the expenses.
Tuition she needed to pay.
A place she needed to stay.
Everything else she minimized.

One muffin a day
Divided in half
One half for lunch, the other half for dinner.

Oh, how hard it was for her to walk by the cafeteria!
The smell of French Fries teasing every sense in her body:
Her skin smelled it!
Her eyes smelled it!
Her ears smelled it!

So, she kept on studying
To overcome her hunger
To overcome her guilt.

'What Do I Want to Be?'

She decided to become a successful businesswoman
First time she flew in a plane.
It sounded great
Being a successful businesswoman
Making tons of money
Flying around the world.

She started her college with business courses:
Economics
Accounting
Finance
She didn't like it.

So, she signed up for science classes in second year.
Still taking first year classes:
Biology
Chemistry
Physics
She loved it.

But then, there won't be many jobs I can do with a science degree, will there?

So, she changed to chemical engineering.
Third year at the college still taking first year classes:
Thermodynamics
Fluid mechanics
Heat transfer
She loved it even more.

This eventually led her to the field of bioengineering.
She was ecstatic!

She was twenty-seven years old
Finishing her bachelor's degree
Feeling old
Uncertain
Far from a successful businesswoman she had dreamed of.

Her parents worrying
Whether she would ever become useful
People mocking
That she would never become successful.

She kept on going.
Undeterred.
Being laughed at never bothered her.

She just walked the path -
The path of learning!

Graduation

Tears pouring out
Smearing all over her face
Her two most wonderful supervisors next to her
And her parents who always doubted her.

There she was
Receiving her degree, Doctor of Philosophy!

It was a long journey.
A little girl from a small country
Who had no hope for success
Now standing tall
In front of many proud faces.

So many people told her
That she would never make it.
So many days and nights
She thought she would never make it.

She finally had something to show
That she too could reach it
That she too deserved to exist in this world.

The tears of joy
Washing away painful memories
Making room for a…

Bright beginning.

First Paycheck

She waited patiently for her first paycheck:
$70,000 divided by 12 equals to $5,833.33!

She used to live on $1,200 per month
Feeling poor always.

Until that job
Her first job in a big company
Big fat paycheck.

The excitement of earning real money,
Real as in,
Full time professional
In a big corporation!

Colorful balloons floating inside her head
Big apartment
Fancy vacation
New car
Some money for her parents back home.

When the paycheck arrived,
She opened the envelop with exhilaration.
Then, she gasped.
She checked the numbers on the pay statement.

Oh, all those taxes and deductions!

Balloons popping
All at once.

It took her a few days to calm her disappointment.
But still grateful
To have a job she always wanted
And earn a decent living nevertheless.

Bride and Groom

Two people in love
Bride and groom
Holding hands
Smiling.

A happy day
Flowers
Champaign
Wedding cake
And dances!

A special day
Surrounded by all their loved ones
Their parents at their sides
Showering them with all their blessings.

So much laugher
So much love

That was the day
Bride and groom
Became one
Union.

Juggling

She was a new mother
A new mother was she.

Juggling her days, Mondays to Fridays
Until her husband,
Living 600 miles away for his job,
Came home for the weekends.

She was a new mother
A new mother was she.

Her two-year old, a picky eater
Her one-year old, a messy eater
She spent hours feeding the picky one
While cleaning up after the messy one.

She was a new mother.
A new mother was she.

After the daycare drop-off
She ran to her office,
Touched up her makeup,
Tidied up her hair,
Sprayed perfume,
She sat in meetings as confident as she could be
Along with male managers and colleagues.

After the daycare pick-up
She came home with her exhausted children,
Clinging to her legs and crying,
She fed them, cleaned them, put them to bed.

Then she cleaned the house,
Cooked for the next day,
Fired up her laptop and worked
For many more hours after that.

She was a new mother.
A new mother was she.

Her boss popped into her office.
"Can you go to Switzerland next week?" he asked.
"Of course!" She responded.
Then she hurried to find help for her little ones
So that she could make the urgent trip.

Many more trips thereafter
Sweden, Belgium, Spain, China, Puerto Rico…
Flying all over the world
In fancy business class.

She was a new mother.
A new mother was she.

Juggling between her little ones and the job.
Week after week, for many years like that.

Finding Purpose

Her son was barely nine months old.
It started as a harmless cold.

After a few days, his cough became severe.
She took him to see the doctor:
"Let the cold pass"
The doctor told her.

Days did pass, but her son became sicker.
His fever got high, and he vomited often.
She took him to see the doctor again.

The words came from the doctor:

"His lungs are clogged.
He is not breathing well.
That is why he was vomiting."

"He must go to the hospital right now.
I will call **9.1.1**."

She jumped in the ambulance
Alongside with her son.

Busy hands of the paramedics
Hooking up the oxygen mask
Cooling down the body temperature
Comforting gently
Everything her sick child needed.

Sitting in the ambulance,
Looking at her son
And the paramedics
She burst into tears.

Tears of relief!
My son will be ok. He is in good hands finally!

Hopes and gratitude
Warmed her desperate heart.

That was the moment that everything became clear
The purpose of her life
And the path that took her
To the field of bioengineering.

I owe to them
The ones who are saving my son's life right now
And many others like them

I will devote myself to make sure
That their hands will always have medicine they need

Saving lives

Bringing hopes.

Lifetime Opportunity

I came to this company because of you.
You impressed me from the start.
I remember the interview.
You asked me only one question.
"How can you help?"
It was the hardest interview I ever had.

Your knowledge, charisma and focus
Only one question to assess
My competence
Enthusiasm
And readiness.

It was so evident to me
That working for you would be my lifetime opportunity.

And it did.
You created numerous opportunities to
Stretch me
Develop me
Inspire me.

You made it possible
For me to grow so fast
Leading multiple teams across the globe
Making medicines for many people in need.

Working for you was indeed
My lifetime opportunity.

Reinventing

She was our new boss.
We gathered in a conference room to meet her.
Two senior managers by her side
Telling us about the great new future ahead.
We sat in the conference room, unenthusiastically.
She was our third boss in less than two years.

She showed up with a big smile
Enthusiastic to learn about each one of us.
We were skeptical.

Months passed, I got to know her better.
I did not think she would notice me and my work
As she was many levels higher than me.

One day, she told me
"I will help you if you would like."

She then shared her story:
That she too used to have doubts about herself,
But many people helped her overcome them.

She must have seen the ambition inside of me
But I was too insecure to allow myself to recognize it.

First, we worked on improving my body language:
Avoiding direct eye contact
Shoulders cringing down
Hands and fingers fidgeting.

She asked me to practice speaking out loud
In front of a mirror
To improve my posture, showing more confidence.

We worked on correcting my self-image:
Comparing myself with others
Undermining my accomplishments
Feeling sorry for myself.

She spent days helping me identify
The harsh voices inside of my head
Criticizing me constantly.

Then we created plans to pursue my ambition.
She forced me to write down what I wanted to become
In two years
Five years
Ten years.

"Dream big!" she said.

It was absolutely energizing
To be able to allow myself to dream!

Today, I am much more confident now.
More assured.
Because she showed how to reinvent myself
To become what I desire to be.

Chocolate Fountain

It is possible to be successful fast.
Big titles
Fat paychecks
Fancy friends
Luxurious holidays.

The success follows with more successes.
Bigger titles
And fatter paychecks.

When that happens
It feels like
Being in the middle of a giant chocolate fountain.

Bounced up so high
By such powerful sweet force
Coating you
Soaking you
Blinding you
With all the sweetness there is.

But watch out!
The fountain will eventually stop.
Chocolate will harden
Leaving the dark stickiness all over your body and soul.

FALL - WITHER

Birthday

Mom walks into the child's bedroom. It has a big window. The sun is setting outside creating bright orange sky, sending the orange rays into the room, to the bed where the child is sitting. As the mom walks in, the child puts down her drawing book. She's been doodling her favorite flowers, trees and her family. Mom bends down towards the child and gives a kiss on her forehead.

CHILD
Mom, can you not go?
Why do you have to travel so much?
Can they come here to see you instead?

MOM
Oh, my sweetheart, I must go. They need me.
I promise to be back as soon as I can.

CHILD
But it is my birthday tomorrow, and I want you to be here!

MOM
Oh, my sweetheart,
I promise we will have a big birthday party this weekend.

Mom sits down next to the child. Her hand caresses the child's cheek. Child looks away. Tears are filling the child's eyes.

MOM
Oh, my sweetheart, please don't cry.

Silence fills the room. Mom is hugging the child, kissing on her head. Child, still looking away, is breathing heavily.

CHILD
Ok. You go. I know it is important to you.
I wish I become important to you someday.

MOM
Oh, my sweetheart, you are important to me!
I will think of you every single minute.
I love you more than the whole world.

The doorbell rings. Mom hugs the child tight. Kisses her goodbye on her head once more. Rolls her carryon suitcase to the driveway where a limousine is waiting.

When Your Soul Is Speaking to You

Sitting in the backseat of a shiny black limousine
While the black-suited chauffer is driving you
To the airport
So that you can board fancy business class
You look out the window and feel your heavy heart
This is when you know your soul is speaking to you.

Your job title becomes more exotic
More and more people look to you for decisions
Trying to get on to your calendar for meetings
Asking for advice
You find yourself feeling incomplete
This is when you know your soul is speaking to you.

Increasing conflicts with others
People resenting your authority
Passive resistance in their smile
Despite how much you try to show that you care
Unspoken words tell you
That they rather see you go elsewhere
This is when you know your soul is speaking to you.

Coming home from a long trip
No more vibrant cheering of a child running to you
No more hugs and kisses
No more "I missed you, mommy!"
Realizing that you are no longer in your child's life
This is when you know your soul is speaking to you.

Your soul is constantly speaking to you.

Insomnia

Time does stop.

When it does
Everything else stops too.

Even your heartbeat.

Stifling you.

Words of Wisdom

"You can find another job and leave here.
But you are bringing the problem with you.
Wherever you will be,
You will still be facing the same problem.

You are blaming them for your failure,
Failure to understand their needs,
And failure to connect with them.
It is your fierce ambition
Alienating you from everyone else.

Learn to work well with others.
Bring them with you.
Gain their trust.
When you reach mastery in that,
Then you can go anywhere and be successful."

This brutally honest advice
Shocked her.
It opened her eyes.

What Hurts More

Loneliness hurts.
It seeps through your skin
Into your bones.

But what hurts more than loneliness?

Shame.

It burns everything inside
Into
Black
Ashes

She Asked Me If

She had an interesting story:
The story of how she left her small country
To become successful in this big country.

I agreed to work
As her designated executive coach
Many years ago
As her company was investing in her
To make her a world class leader.

She was passionate in learning.
She constantly asked questions.
Her enthusiasm reminded me of my younger days
Thriving to become a person of positive impacts.

Eventually, the coaching sessions ended.
But I stayed with her
As a friend
Committed to help her
As long as she needed me.

One day

She asked me if she could undo the mistakes she made
By explaining to people
That she did not mean to push them so hard.
I told her no.
It was too late.
Once the trust is lost, it is impossible to gain it back.

She moved on to another job,
Found herself stuck between demanding management
And burned-out employees

She asked me if she could tell her employees
That it was not she who was demanding the work
But her management.
I told her no.
She had a duty to be uniting, not dividing.
Find ways to align the management and her employees
In a direction that was right for everyone.

She asked me if she was being a failure
Because she kept stumbling into issues:
Conflicts, resentments, jealousy, anger.
I told her no.
She was not a failure.
What was happening reflected what was inside of her:

Constant criticism of others
The need to prove her self-worth
And obsession over what the society defined as success

I told her that
The time had come
For her
To root out all that negativity out of her
And plant seeds of positivity
One-by-one.

Letter

No, I can't sign that letter, Sir.
Because it does not tell the truth.
Because it is a lie.
No one will get hurt by it, I know.
And it will keep the company strong.

We can dissect the numbers in a million ways.
And the story fits perfectly.
But we both know,
Deep inside in our consciences,
That the letter contains mistruth.

No, I will not sign that letter, Sir.
I will probably lose my job for it.
Because I am not being a team player.
Because I am too black and white.
Because I am disobeying your order.

Take away my autonomy.
Discredit my competence.
Withhold my paycheck.
But you can't take away my integrity.

My integrity -
It belongs to me.

Two Ladies on a Bench

Two ladies sat on a bench
One in a big red sweater
The other in a grey jacket.

It was a gloomy day
Dark clouds moving in fast
The sun disappearing quickly
The fallen leaves fluttering with the wind.

"Looks like it is going to rain," said the grey jacket.
"What is your plan?" asked the red sweater.

"I will quit," said the grey jacket.
"Are you sure?" asked the red sweater.

Silence...

"Be responsible. You have a family to support. What are you going to do for money? And you love your work. Don't run away like that," pleaded the red sweater.

Silence...

Resentful smile on the grey jacket:
"I have everything I ever wanted: money, job, family. But I am most miserable. Isn't that ironic."

"Don't take things so seriously. Loosen up," pleaded again the red sweater.

Silence...

The grey jacket took a big breath
Looking at the fluttering leaves,
"I don't know what the purpose of my life is. What is the point of all of this?"

Silence....

Both sat there for a while.
The rain started to fall.

Respectful Goodbye

I sat in his office
Resignation letter in hand.
Tensions between him and me
Escalating over many months.
He may not have seen this coming,
My resignation.
His plan may have well been to fire me first.

The moment he sent me the email, a few weeks prior,
"I was not copied in this email, and this is not acceptable!"
With a big exclamation mark!

I knew he was going to retaliate.
This might have been the opportunity he waited for.
And when it came, he struck hard.

The power game across multiple senior leaders,
He wanted total control over me
To have an upper hand in the game.
But I was never patient and submissive enough
To obey all his orders.

Sitting across the table from my boss,
With my resignation letter in hand,
We both knew
How much he tried to control me
How much I refused to let him.

Mist of anger and frustration
That he held against me
That I held against him

And our heartfelt regret
That we had to come to that point.

It was a respectful good-bye between two professionals.
And we went our separate ways.

Last Day

It will be a hard day.
A meeting coming up.
Meeting with my team members to say goodbye.

What do I tell them?
Everything will be great, and good days are coming?
That is fake.

Maybe I can I tell them everything
Orders
Conflicts
Politics
That is disingenuous.

Should I just skip the meeting?
That is irresponsible.

The sun is coming up
Over the bright blue sky filled with white cotton clouds
And I am sitting here quietly
Contemplating.

The memories of good times and bad times,
Realizing that
This will be my last chance to see their faces.

I will meet them.
I will answer the question.
"No, I don't know what I will do yet."

I must have courage.

Perhaps that is why this is happening,
My selfish ego too proud to acknowledge my faults

Too pretentious to admit

That I am lost.

WINTER - REST

Meditation

Darkness exists because I...
Because I insist on the light.

It is me.
My own self.

Creating the darkness.

Judging bad people.
Admiring good people.

Without realizing that
It is I
Who contain both.

Raindrops

Here you are --
Drop, drop, drop
In the mist of morning sun
Birds chirping that the day has begun.

Your gentle hand
Healing yesterday's thunderstorm
Softly caressing the debris scattered all around.

You are the magician
Transforming into endless forms and shapes.
You are the ocean
You are the clouds
You are the glaciers
You are me--
The trees, and
All other living things on this planet.

You must have seen it all
How the earth evolved
How we the humans constantly fall.

Maybe that is why you keep coming to us
Trying to open our clogged conscience.

Here you are --
Drop, drop, drop
In the mist of morning sun
Embracing me with a gentle hum.

Desire

It is inside all of us
Invisible yet powerful force.

It may appear as our desire for
Success
Love
Fame

Even
Sacrifice,

Driving us to be
Successful
Beautiful
Impactful

And
Helpful,

Only to leave us with emptiness
And regrets.

The truth is,
There resides something else deep down,
Something more profound
Underneath it all
Invisible yet powerful force

Our desire

TO.BE.SEEN!

Would That be Ok

The swearing words popping through my mouth
When I spill water all over my night table -
Would that be ok?

The angry words erupting through my mouth
When my husband comes home late on my birthday -
Would that be ok?

The cynical words slipping through my mouth
When the kids forget to pick up their socks -
Would that be ok?

The resentful words sneaking through my mouth
When I feel the emptiness inside that refuses to go away -
Would that be ok?

I know the words matter.
I know the thoughts matter.

But no matter how hard I try
There comes a time when I snap -
Uttering words that I shouldn't

Perhaps YOU would be ok
That I lose my temper like that from time to time
That YOU will still smile
And watch over me
As I am trying to control my tongue
With all my mighty effort every day.

Voice

Someone is knocking on my door
Trying to come inside.

Who are you?

I am you,
And I am already inside.

I look around.
There is nobody but
Solemn darkness.

I Almost Lost You

I never realized
How many nights you cried yourself to sleep
Wishing that I would stay
That I did not have to travel so much.

I almost lost you
Because I was too busy pursuing my selfish dreams.

I never realized
How forgiving you were
When I came home with stress and frustration
Criticizing you for endless trivial things

I almost lost you
Because I was punishing you for my faults.

I never realized
How accommodating you were
Trying to follow all my unrealistic demands
Even though you were on the verge of breaking

I almost lost you
Because I was using you to find my happiness.

It was your gentle hugs
Your silent tears
And your sacred heart
That pulled me out,
Out of my selfish destruction.

I am forever grateful
That you pulled me out

That you did not let me lose you.

Letter to You from My Open Heart

I was young striving for glorious fame
Fearlessly pursuing dangerous power game.
You must have seen many like me
Always finding others to blame.

There you were
With years of wisdom and lore

You said to me firmly,
"As you move up,
Those external praises will cease.
Criticisms and jealousies will rise.
That is when
You must find your inner fortitude."

You watched me fall over and over again
Patiently waiting for my ego to abstain

Every time I fell, I came running
And you carried me through another beginning.

Your guidance
Your patience
And your assurance

This is how you showed me
That life is not about achieving.
Instead, life is about helping!

Being there for another person.
Keeping faith in another person.
Just like what you have been doing for me
All those years.

So I write this letter to you
From the bottom of my heart
To express my heartfelt gratitude.

I will always hold
The valuable lesson you showed
To help someone someday
As you have done for me.

3:00 a.m.

Truth comes to you at 3:00 a.m.
When all is sleeping
In the most solemn silence
And darkness.

It comes to you then.
All there is within you
Anger
Jealousy
Shame
Regrets
Fear...

FEAR!

All come to you then
Swirling all over you like a thousand bees.

There is no place to run.
You let it purge.
Let it sting you.
All over you.

It is absolutely excruciating.
But you can't run.

For days, weeks and months
You just sit there
Defenselessly.

Then
Slowly
The bees disappear
One by one.

This is when
Silence arises within you.
And stillness.

You can see clearly in darkness.
You can hear clearly in silence.

Liberating you.
At last.

Receiving Love

My dear sweetheart,
Let me tell you a story
Of a girl whom nobody loved.

Her mother was poor.
She worked day and night.

The little girl wanted a nice pair of shoes.
She wanted a fancy lunch box
Just like her friends at school.
Her mother always said no.

This little girl believed her mom did not love her.
There was no one who loved her.
She meant nothing to anyone in this world.
She never cared how much her mother sacrificed for her.
She was always sad and lonely.

Many years passed by,
She cultivated a bitter heart.

My dear sweetheart,
Please don't make the same mistake as that girl.
She lost many years by rejecting her mother's love
Because it did not come in the way she wanted
Hurting herself and many others around her.

Love will come to you in many different ways.
Some may say unkind words to you.
Some may not help you.
Love them the same wholeheartedly.

Then the day will come
You will tell a different story to your little girl
"Let me tell you a story
Of a girl whom everybody loved…"

When I Am No Longer Here

There will be a day when
The sun will rise
And I am no longer here.

The freshness of the morning dew.
The harmony of singing bird.
The Illumination on the treetops.
Everything will be the same except for
I will no longer be breathing with them.

I will have let go of this body
Returning it all back to Mother Earth.
I will no longer remember
All my days of happiness and sadness.

But I hope that I will always carry with me
My love for this life
Where heaven and hell exist within -

And it is all up to me,
My words and actions,
Determining where I belong each day.

And then...

A new spring arrived
Melting away the frozen

A vibrant new sprout
Gracefully Risen

Acknowledgements:

I would like to express my sincere thanks to all the people who helped me, taught me, guided me. I would not be who I am today without their incredible support. I am indebted to each one of them.

I am forever grateful for my loving parents, my brother, my husband and my two children. They have been most patient and loving throughout my wild adventures.

I would send my special thanks to my sister, who encouraged me to write this book. She has always been my greatest mentor, critique and cheerleader in my entire life.

I would like to thank Dr. George Martin, who provided valuable suggestions and corrections for this book.

Younok Dumortier Shin, Ph.D., M.B.A., was born and raised in South Korea. At age 19, she left for Canada, where she completed her education in Doctor of Philosophy, Chemical Engineering specialized in Bioengineering. She then moved to the United States, where she has been devoting her time in developing and delivering medicines.

Outside of her professional career, she works closely with organizations teaching healthy living and mindfulness, helping people maintain physical and emotional wellbeing.

She co-authored *Ionic Surfactants and Aqueous Solutions: Biomolecules, Metals and Nanoparticles,* and published many research articles in scientific journals. *Four Seasons* is her first poetry book.

Currently, she lives in New Jersey with her husband and two children.

Email: yshin@alaired.com
LinkedIn: @Younok Dumortier Shin
Instagram: @alaired_younok
Facebook: @Alaired

ISBN 978-0-578-77108-3

www.ingramcontent.com/pod-product-compliance
Lightning Source LLC
Chambersburg PA
CBHW031410040426
42444CB00005B/497